THIRD

VOICE

ALSO BY RUTH ELLEN KOCHER

Ending in Planes

Goodbye Lyric: The Gigans & Lovely Gun

domina Un/blued

One Girl Babylon

When the Moon Knows You're Wandering

Desdemona's Fire

Ruth Ellen Kocher

3 THIRD VOICE

TUPELO PRESS | NORTH ADAMS, MASSACHUSETTS

Third Voice.
Copyright © 2016 Ruth Ellen Kocher. All rights reserved.

Library of Congress Cataloging-in-Publication Data available upon request.
ISBN: 978-1-936797-73-8

Front cover designed by Ann Aspell. Text designed by Dede Cummings.
Cover and interior art: Nina Chanel Abney, "Untitled" (acrylic, spray paint,
collage on board, 18 x 36 inches). Used with permission of the artist (http://www.
ninachanel.com).

First paperback edition: June 2016.

Epigraph: Excerpt from *The Autobiography of Alice B. Toklas* by Gertrude Stein,
copyright (c) 1933 by Gertrude Stein and renewed 1961 by Alice B. Toklas. Used
by permission of Random House, an imprint and division of Penguin Random
House LLC. All rights reserved.

Tupelo Press is an award-winning independent literary press that publishes fine
fiction, nonfiction, and poetry in books that are a joy to hold as well as read.
Tupelo Press is a registered 501(c)(3) nonprofit organization, and we rely on public
support to carry out our mission of publishing extraordinary work that may be
outside the realm of the large commercial publishers. Financial donations are
welcome and are tax deductible.

ART WORKS.
arts.gov

Produced with support from the National Endowment for the Arts

Carl Van Vechten sent us quantities of negroes. Besides there were the negroes of our neighbor Mrs. Regan who had brought Josephine Baker to Paris. Carl sent us Paul Robeson. Paul Robeson interested Gertrude Stein. He knew American values and American life as only one in it but not of it could know them. And yet as soon as any other person came into the room he became definitely a negro. Gertrude Stein did not like hearing him sing spirituals. They do not belong to you any more than anything else, so why claim them, she said. He did not answer.

—*The Autobiography of Alice B. Toklas*

Contents

Stump Speech   *ix*

⚹

HOW TO STAGE A MINSTREL SHOW   *2*

CAST   *3*

Skit: Lacy Watches Richard Pryor Talk about Love   4

Sentimental Song: Beneath the Sound Outside, a Child
    Crying, Lacy N. Igga Considers Last, But Most, the Bird   6

NEW JOKES FOR FEMALE MINSTRELS   *8*

Skit: The Sound of Another Woman's Heart Pounding   9

When She Is Awake   II

Olio 42   14

Skit: Paul Robeson on Stein, After   16

Skit: Pearl Bailey and Eartha Kitt Revise Observations
    on the Feeling of the Beautiful   17

Olio 44   19

A MERRY MINSTREL BOOK   *22*

Skit: Lacy N. Igga's Outline of Knowledge   23

Skit: She Looks Up *Parasomnia* but Thinks *Middle Passage*   25

Skit: Lacy N. Igga Takes the Stage   27

READY-MADE   *30*

Olio 65   32

DAT'S WHAT'S DE MATTER   *34*

Skit: Sun Ra Welcomes the Fallen   35

Skit: She Is Asked About the Sublime   37

Olio 34   40

Olio 19   42

She Manifests Her Own Ineffable   44

Olio 23   45

Skit: Diaspora III, or Geordi *The Form* of Space   47

Skit: MLK Jr. and Lieutenant Uhuru Have Coffee and Cake   49

Skit: Malcolm X and Marcus Garvey Walk Their Dogs   51

Olio 13   54

WHEN CORK IS KING   56

Olio 22   57

Skit: Creigh-Z. N. Igga Climbs a Tree   60

DE MELANCHOLY EVOLUTION OF ME   62

[No Saints] One Act   63

First-Part Crossfire   68

When You Say Grotesque   69

Conundrum: Somnus 2   72

Skit: Lacy Teaches the Sublime   74

Skit: Lacy N. Igga Considers, Again, Burke's
    "The Effect of Blackness"   79

Monologue: Eva N. Igga and Neva N. Igga
    Twins Not Yet Imagined   82

Skit: Eva Neva and Neva Neva Igga, Twin Babies Come Late   86

Olio 7   88

*

Afterpiece: In Bed, Lacy Adds Up the Benefits of Not Sleeping   93

Acknowledgments and Notations   95

Stump Speech

It ends with   *do me, baby*   It ends with   *Humpty Hump, Do the Humpty Hump*   It ends with *look at me . . . All day long the same song* because someone changed the spit and spark   *Throw your arms in the air like you just don't care*   It began with the ugly brother who wandered cracked desert   Moorish casting   Bloody feet and nowhere to go   The far off lights   Not Portugal   Not Spain *Here's to everybody who said I'd never amount to anything*   It began with cork bark boiled in murk   It began in the forest

THIRD

VOICE

HOW TO STAGE A MINSTREL SHOW

This book is to every amateur minstrel director what blue-prints are to a builder. Explains modern styles of minstrels and novelty minstrels: how to put the show together; how to organize the troupe and conduct rehearsals; where to get material; the opening chorus discusses first-part, olio, afterpiece, costumes, make-up, scenery, music, publicity, program arrangement, etc.

CAST

Lacy Neva Igga:	....	*Lazy*
Creighton-Zach Neva Igga:	....	*Crazy*
Thayer Nott Igga:	....	*Their Judge*
Mama:	....	*Momma*
Neva Neva Igga:	....	*Picaninny come late*
Eva Neva Igga:	....	*Picaninny come later*
The Woman:	....	*You*
You:	....	*The Woman*
Interlocutor:	....	*Mr. Lit, un-interrogated*

Skit: Lacy Watches Richard Pryor Talk about Love

Lacy touches her chest where the hollow lives The women in the audience laugh loudest When Richard says they are cold ass bitches When a Brother loves When the hurt a man earns makes A man a Man heart-split because His Woman went cruel Touched up on that shit inside him Richard's gold Shoes don't show up on stage Lacy thinks   Lacy thinks   in the dressing room He would have looked down at them and Smiled watching each shuffle under the long Red passion of his trousers walking toward the stage *Women* he says   get they heart broke They cry   *Men*   and he waits for laughs to go shallow   *Men hold that shit in like it don't hurt them Walk around and get hit by trucks*   Lacy touches her chest where the hollow lives Wonders how How anyone survives

Sentimental Song: Beneath the Sound Outside, a Child Crying, Lacy N. Igga Considers Last, But Most, the Bird

The parody of parades on Lacy's bookshelf As a parody Lacy might be But the window An office every parody has In every window of every day A Labrador runs from her owner's feet to the campus quad corner Somewhere something invisible to Lacy lures dog-glee The dog raises her snout to swoops A swallow dips the gnat-cloud with no irony or metaphor No ethos or hyperbole Above the lure invisible First a red spot Then a bounding something The dog parts her jaw Bares her tongue Not as a parody but prostrate deferred pedestrian postured Out of sight The lure

The dog The owner's feet What is missing now besides glee Lacy
posits What is missing Now makes me

New Jokes For Female Minstrels

Note: — The end lady in these jokes is addressed by name, but any name can be substituted, and the same can be done with The Woman; the funnier the name used the better.

Lacy. — *I understand you hab been out West.*

The Woman. — *Yes, went everywhere, saw everything.*

Lacy. — *Well, what impressed you most?*

The Woman. — *Well, I think I was most impressed by the sunrise.*

Lacy. — *'Scuse me, dat was impossible.*

The Woman. — *Why impossible?*

Lacy. — *'Cause the sun don't rise in the West.*

Skit: The Sound of Another Woman's Heart Pounding

Lacy opens her eyes and realizes she's the dream another Woman
dreams   The Woman can sleep   but Lacy cannot   The next
day seems uninterested   Lacy stands next to it   The way you
stand next to someone at a bus stop   Looking Around
Smiling closed-lipped   What to do she says Wandering inside the
head of a Woman   It doesn't matter who She is   There is a
man wearing a green sweater   The Woman dreams of him
The green sweater walks away and takes him too   Lacy knows
they are not the same dream   He is long-haired   His tattoos
decide to stay in the room   Tomorrow saddles up   The

morning turns away and becomes its own burden   I can't sleep
Lacy says   Says to the lamp which says nothing

When She Is Awake

Red velvet cake is my favorite cake the Woman thinks while she waits for the mail   Her robe doesn't fit but it is the robe She wore all night in her bed   Some kind of purple   Some kind of cloth   Some scent of herself over a scent of detergent Mostly she thinks this funny   All night in her bed she imagined there was a man in a green sweater   She imagined his hair was locked   His breath was bad   She imagined he snored and she could not sleep   She finds the man funny too as dark things make you feel a dark lift inside you   To say dream is a risk and means to be part of something   I am never part of she thinks I

am bored with becoming something   I am bored with becoming
something terse   Reaching toward Away from not enough
The Woman watches late night TV   The yellow and orange
slanted roofs of Ipanema segue black swans in a pond easily
The Woman thinks I have a name   I have never seen a black
swan   The red velvet of red velvet cake makes The Woman feel
as though she eats Botticelli's Madonna Adoring the Child with
Five Angels   There is no man she thinks there is no man there is
no man there is no man there is no Woman in my bed and she
should say *I am alright* but she isn't   The red velvet makes The
Woman feel as though she's eating Botticelli's Madonna and Child
with an Angel or Caravaggio's Sacrifice of Isaac or Caravaggio's
John the Baptist in the Desert   The Woman eats Caravaggio

everything   She takes her lazy robe inside   She takes her
slippers which are slippers inside   Red velvet steeps the red of
baroque An ordinary thing The Woman mumbles though   The
woman she dreams cannot hear her

Olio 42

The inner ear is full of horses, snails, and vestibules, is a trumpet
which implodes   The inner ear spies on your heart   The
inner ear wants to be shut in   The inner ear and the outer ear
are two ends of a set of cups   The inner ear is most aware of
not sleeping in the dark, is sheet and pulse, is fan whir and hum
and dog and the over-thought woodpecker comes back just before
the sun comes up knowing the gutter calls him at a greater distance
increasing his odds to mate   The inner ear fades and the eyes
devise the day as it slowly disrobes at the window pink and shy

The ear is not gone   The ear and the eye come together   The
ear and the eye hear cloud bark engine the trees saying shoo

SKIT: PAUL ROBESON ON STEIN, AFTER

She's interesting enough to play herself over and over again in indie films that aim to strike the pose of that generation of interest at the moment if the profile necessitates a tortured sort of soul though now she is thin in her good looks her beard grows in dark and faint balancing the delicacy of her face the exception a naturally furrowed brow against an obvious masculinity.

Skit: Pearl Bailey and Eartha Kitt Revise Observations on the Feeling of the Beautiful

Whether we love it or hate it is irrelevant to its worth. We have heard more women call women whores than we have heard men call women whores. We have more light than we know what to do with. Live with it. Some time ago, a Woman asked us for five women we loved and five women we hated and five women we hated to love . . . or maybe five women we hated and five women we loved and five women we loved to hate . . . or both. We haven't been able to answer. We're trying not to sing too easy green and violet veins meaning moth-winged flower or would it be worse to say bloom? The shackled hardwood, the ribs of the house, the ribs of a huge beast, the ribs of a fossil, the ribs of a thing destined to be stone. We call ourselves *Away*. Stranded is a place not a thing.

She' s the queen of Neo-Soul   Slow it down   Hey
Suddenly I'm standing   What do you want from me   You
make me want to leave   Look   It's not about music
There were three young orphans   Four   But about that
Make it disappear   The truth will vanish with them   The truth
has your word   The truth is almost   Hey   Don't be so
dramatic   They make fortunes building bombs   The stone
age is before us   Get outta here   Go on   The story won't
get out   It's not about music   It's not about making
something that makes something else   She snaps her fingers but

the earth quakes   She   *ah*   *ah*   *ahhhhs*   but He still
came home   She sways a sway we don't know how to name
When you want your horizon to work, you'll celebrate it first
There were four orphans but you don't remember their names
Suddenly, they're gone   You don't have to pay a cent   Put
that money in your pocket   She sings for free   She knows that
Truth is ancient and extinct   She knows there are things that can
change you forever   They were not orphans   They were not
a church   In the darkest times, the canyon is unexpected and
still there   The canyon is in her belly and full of C notes   The
canyon is an assailant   The story won't get out   The truth
refuses to name a source   Slow it down   No one talks about

the truth anymore   Suddenly, you're standing .   Goodbye
Don't come back

A MERRY MINSTREL BOOK

Over a hundred pages of endmen's jokes, cross fire dialogues, conundrums, comic verse rapid repartee, talking skits minstrel monologues, and stump speeches, a veritable storehouse of burnt cork comedy, of great aid in getting up a funny entertainment of almost any description. Worth many times its cost to the director who is in search of stuff that has not been worked to death . . .

SKIT: LACY N. IGGA'S OUTLINE OF KNOWLEDGE

The television gives Lacy longing on 36 channels heartbreak on 12 mourning on all the rest sun casts shadows right now sweet late birds see a moon Lacy dreams on both sides of her bed Her longing sleeps too Metastasis on the air double noted death and petunias a third Bug spray fourth The molded murk of rain Drink as much water as you can Sit straight when you look at the moon at which the birds do not look Don't bother counting Blades of grass will not grow under your feet Lacy's mother long ago would call All the children home The summer calls Children come home Lacy

clocks the smooth face The moon look   Look at the way Look
at the moon

SKIT: SHE LOOKS UP *PARASOMNIA* BUT THINKS *MIDDLE PASSAGE*

The evening first waves and shackles smells of rotting wood, skin, shit sea stink 1-800 numbers   miracle juicers flowers in long boxes a BDSM slave collar that can pass for vanilla jewelry bought boxed shipped delivered to Lacy's door   A waking dream about captivity   Sleep-shopping   Anybody's guess   Later, she will explain that the moon is cliché   The moon is groggy gray and nothing else   Not a slave ship   Nor one hundred and thirty three bodies caught in the rapture of enormous deep pervasive blood-red drowning in a Turner painting   The moon is a paradigm for sublime disposal   or Baldwin hissing *rope, fire,*

torture   Who do we think we are   The moon is a map   Do
not close your eyes   Lacy doesn't   Do not close your eyes
Lacy cannot be anything but awake   A student struggles against
the first eighteen years of her life   Her hand   reaches highest

Skit: Lacy N. Igga Takes the Stage

Lacy's regalia is smarter than a mop   maybe smarter than
Fitzgerald's *negroes*   and the *yolks of their eyes*   maybe Burke's
black bodies   those *vacant spaces*   maybe not   Lacy's smile
is whiter than a whale   if sublime singularity   smells like sea
salt and despair   Stein's mulatta drops it like it's hot   all *white*
blood strong   all *wandering* and *dark*   Jefferson's *brutes*
Jefferson's *bucks*   Jefferson's *bile that blackens negro skin*   that
absence of *civility*   maybe that music that never played in a play
about music   That Lit dude who cramps her disembodied
aesthetic   Taps that fat ass draped in pomp   slaps that *broad*

glow of negro sunshine   Dang   there's Stein again   Work that
Melanctha   Black Vamp   Sweet-ee   *Mammy*   Bae   or
nigger nigger nigger   [What book was that?]   Every podium
Every classroom   Lit tips a hat   tips white-face   tips some
kinda black-face   un/molded   un/blued   un/ended
un/hanged   un/turned   un/zipped   Say   Say   Faulkner
Say *bull of a nigger . . . mouth loud . . . filled with teeth like tombstones*
Smile   Smile   Kantian blackness   Hey cork   Hey skin
Lacy thinks   *robed*   thinks *robbed*   thinks *my body*   *a shank*
my body   a body   my body something sometime a promise   my body
something sometime a rot at the edge of the field   the edge of the woods
the edge of the road roped to a tree   sweet and smoldered   Lacy nods
nods   smiles   smiles   silly lazy lazy Lacy lazy lazy   *robed*

robbed   Lit smacks   claps   clasps white gloves   apes his
eyes   gets on his knees   begs for mercy   mercy   yeah, an
audience laughs   yeah, they laugh   listen to this: a rupture
hyenas   high-pitched dogs   high-pitched pack   Lacy thinks
Lacy thinks   *I am tired of making things beautiful*   *I am sugar
cane distilled as fire*   *Do not say Haunted*   Lacy thinks   Lacy
thinks   *Haunted*   *Haunted*   *so difficult unless otherwise engaged
with smiling and nodding*   yo — diplomas for Williams   for *saltpeter
on nigger food*   hey laughter   hey pages   leather and folded
shuffle and snap   smile big   smile haunted   smile feeling
some kinda way   *shake that*   smile curtain   music   smile
music   smile even when no one looks

READY-MADE

A choice of five complete routines, expertly arranged and ready to use, for the convenience of inexperienced amateur minstrel directors and others seeking a modern, properly constructed first part. Instead of being a volume of miscellaneous crossfire from which to pick and choose, each book gives an exact procedure to be followed in staging a sure-fire first-part — complete dialogue and full instructions for action and stage business from rise of curtain to grand finale. These books will prove a salvation for the many amateur minstrel troupes which lack the personal counsel and guidance of an experienced director. Thoroughly professional in style, yet entirely practical for amateurs, and give big opportunity for localized jokes. Written to order especially for troupes wishing to stage an expertly routined show at a nominal cost. Each first-part will consume about one hour and can be used for a troupe of any size, large or small. Music is not included, but the respective song programs can be obtained complete from the publisher.

OLIO 65

A pink sweater not dark but light almost not pink her tongue a
flower which he says isn't pink because no pink exists in nature but
we brought him pink pink everywhere in beer bottles in milk
containers in our hands in bunches everywhere which made him
love us and hate us as we loved him and hated him whose tongue
was not pink in the way you imagine but in the way red fades from
being red although red is not part of this story because red turns
away from pink as a brother turns away from another brother
when a woman is involved and her pink sweater pushes each to
think pink nipple pink lip pink flower in the way Boethius thought

pink flower thinking woman thinking man not thinking to keep the allegorical away because the allegorical does not tolerate pink which is soft and weak because it is nature at its failing because a girl sparkles from her feet to her head in pink backpack scarf gloves because she is too young to understand how pink hates a woman because she is too young to know how pink hates a man

DAT'S WHAT'S DE MATTER

probable meaning:
my deluded frens   *my dear friends*
my disgusted hearers   *my distinguished hearers*
my insignificant frens   *my significant friends*
    (my crazy congregation)

Skit: Sun Ra Welcomes the Fallen

Jupiter means anger. Sun Ra does not. Sun Ra dances the Cake Walk on Saturn's pulpy eyes. If you believe that, I'll tell you another one. The first is 13 and the next is 20. They were not good boys but they were boys. They were boys who died for this thing or that. The next was 16 and the last was 18. One had a cell phone. One had a gun. On earth, a goose opens its chest to a sound. The goose takes the bullet this way. A sacrifice denied to the wind since there is no such thing as sacrifice anymore having succumbed to fever and the millennium. The bullet is all consequence. Sun Ra refuses red — long and high, low and deep. His arms are long enough to embrace them.

Skit: She Is Asked about the Sublime

And says   *not Berryman*   but then what?   What is it about this
kind   What about this kind   Is it   That makes disagreement
So   Disagreeable   meaning   that kind of Woman red winged
floating in a field beneath a mountain range not any one in
particular but white peaks extraordinary incapable rendering
unknown mathematical vision of rock and ice all the same a horror
the mind cannot comprehend   meaning articulate   *That's why*
we hired you   nice (skin)   *Your hair looks better straight*
knowledge-able   *You seem so . . . angry*   Look at her   Just a

little daft   *Someone who uses the word "reference" as a verb*   Just a
little bit slow   *This is not about race. It's about . . . aesthetics*
Another voice says   *We wanted someone else*   whether the
substance of knowing that voice matters or not   *The effort to charm
becomes painful and is felt to be wearisome*   She marks this page in
her book   The inter-objective way to say blackness is *the wind causes
the chimes to sound   The wind causes the doorway to moan* or   She's
drunk   She's lazy   She's no Mr. Bones   Don't be angry   *I
don't know what Primitivism has to do with anything*   She is *an embodied
form of difference   The sublime body displaced for aesthetic vision*   Lacy
laughs too loudly   and someone says   *Bipolar or Booze*   Lazy
Lacy   all Baldwin   all Brooks   Misunderstanding is
understandable and will go away   Smile smile smile   Mammy

Hours Tuesday 2–4   Nodding Smiling implies she understands
Smiling especially   Dispels rumor

Olio 34

A time ago no one smiled in photographs and the absence of a smile meant that the mouth was serious and so the face was serious and so the hair and so the arm and so on There was a red velvet chair Behind the mouth there may have been teeth or may not have been teeth There was a red velvet chair There may have been an utterance deep in the throat an echo of the chest a small recessed word clamoring to traverse the line of teeth the line of lips There may have been an unnoticed happiness that came from a simple thing The bread has risen The ice has thawed The cellar is filled with potatoes There was a red velvet chair A time ago not smiling in a photograph meant that sepia spoke first meant the corset held its breath meant a dog had died perhaps perhaps not meant many rooms perhaps or not meant servitude maybe not A time ago the smile was inconsistent and could not be trusted There was a red velvet chair A time ago the smile was an outlaw the smile was an open curtain the smile was the world seeping in the way a keyhole allows the outside in though no one sees it There was a red velvet chair in which no one sat Behind the mouth there may have been melting snow may have been the violins that tell us what we should feel There was a red velvet chair where someone would not sit There may have been a watch that did not tick A time ago sepia said no posture said no ruffles said no no the chair said no the phosphorous said stay said still said where can you go

You can't learn to ignore [   ] Which means each color all in movement morning decreasing endlessly and noisy in a way only solved and quieted by vodka or walking. [   ] is your face. [   ] is your hand. [ ] reconfigures a white expanse. [ ] assumes a black expanse. [   ] has forgotten your name. You're standing in sweet grass. You're weaving a Gullah basket. [   ] is a dreadlock. [   ] is ashy. [ ] is a book. [ ] is a rope. [ ] is where you've been or what you choose or what you kill. [   ] is better than your body. Like California. Arizona. Colorado, and . . . [   ] is better than that. You, too. You're amazing. You're better than butter and sunshine.

Your heart throbs begonias. You're summer sultry easing   You won't give it up.

A. The Sublime
B. Terror
C. All of the above

She Manifests Her Own Ineffable

Other than the intricacies of the creak sky blackness that opens against the horizon A horizon not imagined as any way to anything Crouch in some ways recessing against a train of No a well of intentions and cliché A well with a surface that you understand to be water but reflects not me but you not her or him or him but you You with your eyebrows crooked like night bending through a stairwell Not her or dried egg white on the counter Between the first day and the Second day Other Intricacies of royal Sunshine say Sunshine again and again until it is all consonant and vowel Nothing Else Nothing not there or there either Here

Olio 23

Who does the road know   Who does the road know when the
sun sits on its toe   Who does the road know now that the fence
has fallen   Now that the fence has fallen where do the doe go
Now that the fence has fallen where do the birds sit   The birds
sit on a wire   Everyone knows the birds sit on a wire   Do the
birds know the fence is gone   Does the wire know the road is
long   The road leads to a star   The star is never and always
found   The doe does not know   The birds sit in a row on the
fence that is fallen   The birds don't know or the birds don't care
or the birds as birds think only sit, think only fly   The birds think

eat   The fence curves a line like the road   The fence and the road
follow the same path   Neither reach the star   Neither knows where
the doe go

Skit: Diaspora III, or Geordi *The Form* of Space

Geordi La Forge cannot be trusted, his tin-thin hollow galaxy arc
gaze gestures chin up epic displacement Kunta in space   who
cannot become hero   ask   (servitude evolves the Master
the Master evolves the slave) do not be deterred by chocolate-
love-mista-street-sage-fuzzy-pimp-Mandingo-noble-savage-savant
—*that cat women* want black-muled love buffalo-ape-uniformed
and approved   out there in space   Buddha knows   the
medieval story goes such that Monkey somersaults not to the end
of the universe but to the infinite pillars of Buddha's left hand,
fingers spread wide as desert but the poor cudgeled trickster cannot

understand the not-so-finite space of wisdom   proud Geordi
says, *make it so*—stars crouched like white syllables low in his throat
ivory grinned hubris twinkling

Skit: MLK Jr. and Lieutenant Uhuru Have Coffee and Cake

Uhuru's cat eyes extend nearly to her Temples   Each sweep of lid makes small gusts through the diner So the short waitress With the mod' green nails and Nancy Sinatra hair spends much Of the morning closing then re- Closing The swinging steel-framed door Uhuru lowers her eyes to her cup Raises her hand Removes a dove from her mouth   The dove says   *Dismantle*   *Dwell* *Expanse*   Uhuru reaches for sugar   The dove says   *Dystopia* *Brute*   *Home*   The dove says *Domain*   The dove says *Grace means to do so*   She raises her hand   puts the dove back in her mouth Raises her eyes to meet the eyes swelling in front of

her   Martin looks over her red uniformed shoulder   He looks
through the window past the white Cadillac hood   over the
mint green roof of the Lorraine Hotel   The trees bud   ripen
and fail in the course of two   perhaps three stop-light
revolutions   *In space*   Martin says in an oratory whisper as
the waitress refills his coffee   brings Uhura's side of cream
In space   we need someone to plant orchards   He squeezes her hand
as the sun angles her curves away   Leans into his own breath
Someone   he says   *and I trust you*

Skit: Malcolm X and Marcus Garvey Walk Their Dogs

They sniff the electric air They pant in their paths They are not devils then they are They are foreigners and then they are not They stop and see the bush, the leaves, the bird They pull at the leash The bird flies left and their heads turn They are Mammies They are Silver Foxes They are obvious They are white devils They kill and are being killed They are black-faced They are bitches They are bulls They are horses and now they're not They are hunting They are born and bred They leave and then they return They shoot They burn bodies tied to trees They laugh They bark at the moon They adjust their ties They fasten up signs They smell their own asses

They buck against the leash They are coons They bite They whimper in corners They plot They burn lawns They run fields and the red wings fly away They jump trees and the squirrels run away They measure numbers They count by tens They bite through bone They write down names They chase death in the day They chase death in the night They are waiting They swim in lakes and run down birds They pant their noses to the ground They dig They knock on doors in the middle of the night They call the police They run for joy it seems They run for their lives it seems They are happy with air and eating They are happy neither now nor ever They write letters to senators They speak in tongues They are wary of strangers Bird ---------- --   --   - -   They pause at a scent They wait They make long speeches and now they don't They stand guard and now they don't They are quiet They are thirsty They can't smell upwind. They don't see it coming.

Olio 13

That's your birthright. Keep it going. Last thing I see is a former friend with her arms held wide. She was so stark. So much out of love all these years. Teach me grace and humility. God bless. Your time has just begun. The grown man cries and says he's a grown man so everyone knows how unusual this mess. Go big. Let's face it. We know what kind he be. Much more than a strong-arm. Much more than a lost cause. If there's a place you'd rather be, no place is off limits. Think lemons and oranges arranged neatly in bowls. She's a mystery and he's waiting. She's a black pebble and laughter. What a reception. She knows him beyond the river stones. She hears him beyond the articulation of suburban walls. You like it, don't you? Say, please . . . You hear applause and it's as beautiful as cliché. You hold his head like she would. You're a black feather and ignite him.

WHEN CORK IS KING

A rich store of bright, snappy material for building up a minstrel show and affording lively chatter for first-part and olio. Conveniently arranged with subdivisions under which are assorted first-part cross fire, end gags and comebacks; end jokes for female minstrels; minstrel miscellany including verses, conundrums and short bits of catch humor; seven dandy monologues; three fast blackface skits . . .

Bachata, Balboa, Ballet, Ballroom, Basque, [hear that] Belly, Bhangara, Black Bottom, Bomba, Boogaloo, Boogie Woogie, Bop, Bossa Nova, Boston, [the hours are saying] Breakaway, Breakdancing, Bump and Grind, Bugg, Bunny Hop, Butoh, Butterfly, Buyo, Cakewalk, Calypso, Carol, [the hours say] Castle Walk, Chaconne, Cha Cha Cha, Charleston, Chicken Dance, Chula, Clogging, Clowning, Conga, Contra, Crunk, Disco, Doublebugg, [hear] Electric Slide, Fandango, Farruca, Folk, Foxtrot, Freak, [back to boogie woogie] Funk, Galop, Grind, Grizzly, Gumboot, [the hours are saying shhhh] Habanera, Hambo, Headbang, Hip Hop,

Hokey Pokey, Hora, Hula, Hully Gully, [the hours say] Irish, Jig, Jive, Jump, Koftos, Lambada, Lap, [back to boogie woogie] Limbo, Lindy Hop, Line, Lyric, Mambo, Mashed Potato, Maypole, Merengue, Minuet, Monkey, [restless] Mosh, Nutbush, Odissi, Para Para, Peabody, Peewee, Persian Pop Lock and Drop, [hear that] Pogo, Polka, Pony, Punk, Push, Quadrille, Rain, Rapper, [the hours are saying] Reggae, Robot, Rumba, Salsa, Sarabande, Schoolcraft, Sequence, Shag, Shake, Shim Sham, Shimmy, Shuffle, [shhhh] Skank, Skip, Slip, Slowfox, Step, Swim, Swing, Suzie Q, [the hours are saying] Tango, Tap, Tik, Tranky Doo, Troika, Turf, Tumba, Twist, Two Step, Universal, Upa, Valeta, Volte, Waltz, Watusi, Western, [hear that] Hear that, [again] Whip, Worship,

YMCA, Zorba, Zouk, Zumba [shhhhhhhh] [Boogie Oogie Woogie]

Skit: Creigh-Z. N. Igga Climbs a Tree

Lacy's mother yells up *Black folks don't sit in trees* so Creigh-Z laughs first   Blast narrative from each branch the pieces come back alive themselves   *Can't be helped*   Lacy thinks   Lacy-Creigh's mother yells 'Neva' then all children run home at once Lacy Neva Igga   Creighton-Zach Neva Igga   Neva Neva and Eva Neva Igga   afro knots black ink twin babies come late Creigh-Z thinks *The dark is an object*   Creigh-Z sits in a tree carrot cake & 7-Up on the belly watching birds   Birds singing in no time   *Cold out too*   whispers the breaking branch Creigh-Z. N. Igga laughs at the fall all the way down so much not Adam

So much vertigo amused at flight Creigh-Z or His lack of flight
Lacy thinks Creigh-Z   Lacy thinks *Falling can't be helped*   Lacy
thinks *don't say Icarus*   Laughing   she would not have thought
to do

DE MELANCHOLY EVOLUTION OF ME

Blackface monologue. Timing 20 minutes. A broken-down negro actor tells the side-splitting story of his experience with an Uncle Tom's Cabin troupe that turned itself into a circus side show in a vain effort to keep from stranding. A Kansas cyclone dealt the final blow. Fine material for a clever negro impersonator.

[No Saints] One Act

You're waiting for the end-gag. You're talking to the newsstand guy who's really looking at your breasts which he'll call tits when he talks to the next guy and the gum you want is gone A case behind the prologue Which is the counter of which he's oblivious He's on your tits The woman next to you is safe in sweats obscured made boy in her hips and chest With those long lines of velour and so he doesn't notice her Though you're thinking Parode and do not say so when she leans in front of you puts down her drink puts down her chips puts down what must be put down [could she love a cat] and His gum chewing and the register beeping Still your gum on the other side of the counter still wrapped   None of this is beautiful or steeped in the freedom narrative you know it should have That which lends itself to everything If the voice in your head would simply say *whisper*   say *potato sack*   Don't speak *Don't speak*   None of this can fill a chicken coop nor make milk for the hungry If there were a voice you answered inside your head She would ask   *Bathing?*   The porter looks at you   But sweat-suit speaks to him Hair swings 'round the shoulder What you call   *the way white girls do it*   Horse mane and pretty and shake even the foot hooved Maybe also a shake of the neck and the finger without a ring Which then you lament her lament of not having [who loves her] Which is obvious   None of this apologizes for men hanging from trees   Or Louis Allen or Jimmie Lee Jackson who no one

remembers like Emmett Till before Emmett Till was remembered
And right there you should think Heidegger [can she love the sour
smell of sex] Why neither he nor she could know Fascist but then
What   *Agon Agon*   lookin' for sunshine spit-shine moonshine
If there were a voice in your head besides your own She would say
air tank   She would say *you are drowning* The pink sweat-suit has
print across her ass as all the pink sweated sweat-suits seem to have
lately as though each ass were an orange or a peach Which your
chest is not Neither written nor sweat-suited and at which [could
she love a violet which won't bloom] The register man still stares
Like ownership is invisible Not unlike the spouse she doesn't have
or hides having or has lost whether she still looks for a body or
not and whether [or whether] or not she knows that Parabasis

means she is a comedy or that Epilogue in her hands feels like Tragedy also None of this appreciates rows of soybean The voice of the woman you cannot imagine not in your head would say *razor* would say *you are dull*   None of this accounts for all of the people you will never know because fields had to be and the houses had to be And the profits of strangers suddenly means you cannot console her You cannot say you lost something too You cannot agree with her that the man at the register is a wise-ass wearing Tommy Hilfiger cologne which you can buy at Wal-Mart anyway None of this would grow if you watered it If you spoke to the voice in your head you could finally understand but would discover a different language The porter walks closer Almost bumps you with his cart to let you know he's noticed and so Doesn't notice Distract everyone who is not speaking Fan your face Unbutton one button and fan your neck None of this can be eaten by the truly hungry The porter imagines *Uppity bitch Big tits* But the newsstand guy also How he loves the Exode of fluorescent light How it makes him gut-strong   keeps the counter in front of him Love that woman If you can but your shoulder bag is too heavy Love Love that woman if you can but her hands are too empty You end up talking to the Chorus which is the newsstand guy Who you realize just now has nowhere to go

First-Part Crossfire

Lacy: *Shhhhhhhhhhh   We're not supposed to be   in   here*

Creigh-Z: *Shhhhhhhhhhh   You might wake us up*

WHEN YOU SAY GROTESQUE

You are the Woman who understands you dream the life of another Woman who shuffles inside your head Who imagines the window swallows Everything You can laugh about this Windows are greedy The reflection of trucks belongs to them When you say grotesque do you mean Grotesque like In Ohio Dresses mean women busy With everyone's business There is no sex There is no touching There is No one to sit back rubbing his chin saying, *Ah, grotesque* If you smirk, you know You can laugh, again so every character trapped Named in the mind that imagines them *Are those blue curlers in your hair Orange is a brave color* Can you brave orange

Can you brave orange with gray slate   Can orange be introduced
to itself   See how orange ends up breathless How it dies
When the light changes they go away and here you should ask, if
you're paying attention, who "they" might be   Your mind
assures you that You cannot leave   There is one more scene
The mind doesn't know who they might be   The mind imagines
recycled paper   That aluminum cylinder thing with a red handle
someone cranks to sift flour and you didn't want to sift flour then
But you want to sift flour   Now   The grotesque has   No
graffiti because graffiti is beautiful you should not say beautiful
No one imagined   Swimming pools are television screens,
eventually   Sales at H&M don't exist either   That Woman
Who wonders about everything   Milk Traffic Frozen Food
You are that Woman who wonders

Whether to make eye contact or not when someone passes by
Someone who you do not know The grotesque is not which is
where you live The notion that everything is *alright* like the couch
receives you from the outside where Each street was unfortunately
out in the world The notion is grotesque Men are not imagined
The face gone wrong you'd like to believe but you're wrong
Wrong   Wrong   Wrong [insert someone else's face here]
Where is the Woman who meringues in Rio de Janeiro who makes
neither lilies nor Wheat nor Thunderbirds nor Drive-Ins in her
head Because she forgets the life in her head   Her sequins forget
their black glint without effort   Here is the Woman who insists
her Dream her Dream is Someone

Conundrum: Somnus 2

You don't think rain   So surprise   There   Rain   Rain
But thunder as longing upsets you   Let it rain or not   Let it
be or not be what you don't think of when you think of a window
that belonged in a flower shop   You can imagine any flowers
you like   Lilies are the best flowers to imagine   Stargazers
are the best kind of lilies   The day breaks in the same way the
night does   Reluctantly   Cowardly   Just easing away . . .
Imagine just easing away   What you rely on betrays you with
no malice   Ice is Ice   Day breaks or night breaks somewhere
quietly somewhere full of sirens & talking   [why

name how Matisse made a yellow curtain when you know yellow is there and blue is here A curtain shrugs separately When someone studies Matisse the curtain is not obvious]   Yellow there Blue here   Everything   Listen just a little   Why should I tell you for everything's sake as though you without knowing me could care   No one listens to a Woman's sleep

SKIT: LACY TEACHES THE SUBLIME

Kant: The Negroes . . . have by nature no feeling that rises above the ridiculous.

Du Bois: And herein lies the tragedy of the age: not that men are poor,—all men know something of poverty; not that men are wicked,—who is good? not that men are ignorant,—what is Truth? Nay, but that men know so little of men.

Kant: Nothing is so opposed to the beautiful as the disgusting, just as nothing sinks more deeply beneath the sublime than the ridiculous.

Du Bois:	There is but one coward on earth, and that is the coward that dare not know.
Burke:	After we have been used to the sight of black objects, the terror abates, and the smoothness of glossiness, or some agreeable accident, of bodies so colored, softens in some measure the horror and sternness of their original nature; yet the nature of their original impression still continues.
Kant:	The inclination to show one's worth to superiors is noble, but to equals or inferiors is contemptible . . .
Burke:	Though the effects of black be painful originally, we must not think they always continue so.

Kant: He whose feeling tends towards the melancholic is
           so called not because, robbed of the joys of life,
           he worries himself into blackest dejection but
           because his sentiments, if they were to be
           increased above a certain degree or to take a false
           direction through some causes, would more
           readily result in that than in some other condition.
           He has above all a feeling for the sublime.

Burke: Black will always have something melancholy in it,
           because the sensory will always find the change to
           it from other colors too violent; or if it occupy
           the whole compass of the sight, it will then be
           darkness . . .

Du Bois: All life long crying without avail, As the water all
           night long is crying to me.

Burke:	Custom reconciles us to everything.
Du Bois:	The cost of liberty is less than the price of repression
Kant:	There are Negroes dispersed all over Europe, of whom none ever discovered any symptoms of ingenuity
Du Bois:	And yet not a dream, but a mighty reality—a glimpse of the higher life, the broader possibilities of humanity, which is granted to the man who, amid the rush and roar of living, pauses
Kant:	Mr. Hume challenges anyone to adduce a single example where a Negro has demonstrated talents
Du Bois:	I sit with Shakespeare and he winces not. Across the color-line I move arm in arm with Balzac and Dumas, where smiling men and welcoming women glide in gilded halls. From out

the caves of the evening that swing between the
strong-limbed earth and the tracery of the stars, I
summon Aristotle and Aurelius . . . and they come
all graciously with no scorn nor condescension.
So, wed with Truth, I dwell above the Veil.

Burke: We have only followed the most leading roads;
            and we shall observe the same conduct in our
            inquiry into the cause of beauty.

Kant: If the relations of beauty are relations of quality
            (identity and difference, contrast, likeliness) then
            no discipline is possible, and even less science, but
            merely criticism.

Du Bois: The price of culture is a Lie.

Skit: Lacy N. Igga Considers, Again, Burke's "The Effect of Blackness"

Lacy N. Igga cannot eat bananas   She cannot eat the bags
around them filled with pesticide and late century ideals
Though Creigh-Z laughs and peels the skin back   She is uppity
Creigh-Z says both out loud and inside his shaved head   like
Uncle Thayer N. Igga's shaved head   Thayer is first a law clerk
and after The Judge   He wears a black robe over his black body
His black object   Lacy thinks   Lacy thinks *some agreeable accident
of bodies so colored softens in some measure the horror and sternness of original
nature*   But Thayer's nights all nights in a row   In books in
books

Creigh-Z shakes his head   Y'all uppity   Remembers Thayer's
face in books and books   He could not eat books Creigh-Z says
Lacy thinks   How much our same story   How much Thayer
wanted when Justice turned in his bed   When she licked his ear
When her blindfold came off and she said   *Daddy I luvs you like
sugar luvs cavities*   When she said *Daddy I need new shoes   I need
my hair did up nice   Daddy do you luvs me   Do you luvs me   Let me
know*   Thayer did not hang himself as others hung or were
hanged   Hanged whether the trees were Money green or leaf
green   Hanged whether the DOW was up or down   Whether
sirens did or did not wail   Lacy thinks   The leaves
Whether money or leaves   Cannot forget hanging   *Black
will always have something melancholy about it*   But still someone
stays hungry

Lacy thinks   Sirens will wail   It is true you cannot eat books
Creigh-Z laughs   The uppity should eat bananas He says   The
uppity should eat bananas and be happy   She cannot eat
bananas or ride a bike that death rides too or alone get on a boat or
enter the woods or imagine very far away herself by herself and so
Lacy cannot   I cannot sleep Lacy says   I cannot *occupy the whole
compass of sight*   I cannot *become darkness*   Creigh-Z scratches his
head   Creigh-Z sticks out his tongue   Creigh-Z gets on his
knees   Opens his arms wide   Sings *Mammy pleeeeeeeez*   Lacy
laughs laughs   Laughs and says   again

Monologue: Eva N. Igga and Neva N. Igga Twins Not Yet Imagined

Mama clicks on the TV chef   *I have to cut my heart very thin to make it tender*   Then   *the pig's ear*   she slaps on the counter Mama knows Apocrypha makes this so   Makes us happy But cliché   *Fuck the list of things you want to do before you die* Mama's punch line   Black again   The face   *Lady Be Fierce* Commit to the line   *Thank YOU*   (on stage The Angry Black Woman hits her mark)   It's all about timing   Mama knows says   *Give Mama a bite of your cookie*

The audience is a laugh   The audience is a buzz   The audience
is a cat call in an empty room   *Art needs to be provocative*
Mama laughs too   The audience is a door closed by someone
not the wind   *I am real*   Mama says from stage   *I am real and
have made somewhere into a door*   Mama says from the stage   The
audience is a slow right turn   *I have made nowhere into a key*
Mama says   *I have made nowhere into a taste*   *You eat me bite by
bite like a red velvet cake with black icing*   The audience is made of
hoof beats   The audience is made of cream   *I am curses*   Mama
says

The audience is an umbrella folding   The audience is an empty
plate   The audience is a wing beating against a window
Mama hits her mark   The lighting is afterthought
Mama is born   Mama dies   Mama is born and means to bare
Twin black babies everyone knows are witchy   Mama touches the
air from which her girls have not yet been imagined   Mama's voice
is vinegar and red dye   Mama's voice is cream cheese icing
Mama says   *When my twin babies pause at wind   You will consume
them   You will kill them   You will shoot them   You will cut them*

You will take them in bites   The audience is clay   The audience is an equation   The audience is a gaping jaw from which a sound comes   from which a moon shines   Mama says surrounded by stage   *You will chew them*   *You will eat their red center*   The audience is no one and everyone at once   Mama says   to no one and everyone at once   *You will gorge on the way each with an eye will punctuate the other's silent sentence*

Skit: Eva Neva and Neva Neva Igga, Twin Babies Come Late

Mama imagines them out of air and hope she keeps in a box
She fills them with everything and nothing   so they keep dying
Then come back   Eva dies first after eating four kernels rat
poison corn   Crunched like candy   Mama in the background
cries over something the window lets out   Again then
Eva's sky tips sideways   Eva Neva walks the gutters on spirit
toes   a pickaninny wonder   a watermelon stripe   an ink
well spilled on concrete   Floating above   Eva watches
her dusty body sprawled on the sidewalk   Mama cries
from something the window lets out   Eva's body makes small
jerks   The jerks push everything and nothing out of her throat
She hears her sister's voice click beneath her   *Poor poor girl*
Wait 'til Mama sees you messed your dress   Neva Neva calls Eva
back to her body as only

Twins can do   So the earth catching up slams the sidewalk into
Eva Neva's face   So hard so hard   So everything and nothing
comes out of her   Neva's shoes she sees at eye level   back
in her body   back to the sidewalk   Neva's shoes specked by
everything and nothing so   Neva's messed too   *You're back*
Neva says   Eva nods   *You are empty*   Neva says   Eva
nods   *Poor girl Poor poor girl*   Neva bends slowly at her waist
Bends slowly beneath something the window let out   Wipes
everything and nothing off her shoes

Olio 7

Everywhere I go   they want to know if it works   The party
doesn't stop until after the show   Any noise is Them setting up
We're with you no matter what   She'll be great   Precaution
and Side effect now mean the same thing   Did you know you
get that for free   Watch her and listen   For now, though
When you need us what you need   How you doing   What do I
need to do   The first thing is talk to somebody   Not your
girlfriends   Speak anonymously if you made the mistake Only
you I'm just saying it's okay You need to hope   Me, too
True   So *alright*   Okay   We're there   More twins
Wow

We're with you   Is this about your twin   I love twins   I'm
getting ready   How do I get him away from his Mama   Who
cares if she's mad   It's not up to the Woman   You might think
twice   Grow up   Step up   Don't miss it

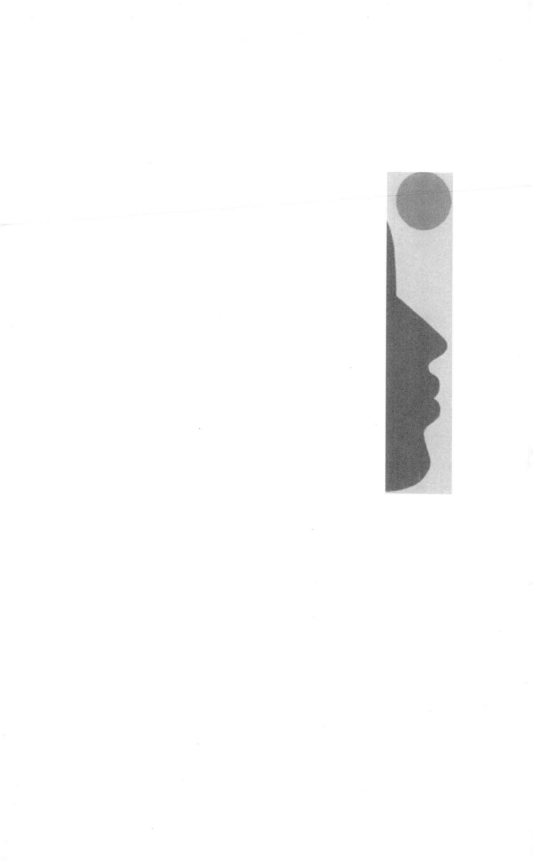

Afterpiece: In Bed, Lacy Adds Up the Benefits of Not Sleeping

1. quiet cannot bore deeper into Than quiet 3 A.M.

2. as though it All were dead

3. the hum

4. the day After the day after the night

5. a girl comes in from Another year so far away it's forgotten except in the dark Full not in the over-used moon but in the forgetting Her lips were very dry Her breath —

6. ...

Acknowledgments and Notations

Poems from *Third Voice* have appeared in *American Letters and Commentary, Coon Bidness, Copper Nickel, The Enemy, IOU: New Writing On Money, Taos Journal of Poetry and Art, TitMouse,* and *Torch,* and in the anthologies *Academy of American Poets Poem-a-Day* and *Best American Experimental Writing 2015.*

Third Voice samples language from Immanuel Kant's *Observations on Feelings of the Beautiful and Sublime,* Edmund Burke's *A Philosophical Inquiry into Our Ideas of the Sublime and the Beautiful,* and W. E. B. Dubois's *The Souls of Black Folk.* Textual artifacts and "ready-made" texts are borrowed from the "how-to" minstrel manuals *New Jokes for Female Minstrels* and *Female Minstrel Jokes* from *Up-to-date Minstrel Jokes: A Collection of the Latest and Most Popular Jokes, Talks, Stump-speeches, Conundrums and Monologues for Amateur Minstrels,* collected and arranged by H. H. Wheeler (Boston: Up to Date Publishing, 1902), and *The Black Vamp: A Blackface Act,* by Arthur Leroy Kaser (Chicago: Nison's Blackface Series, T. S. Denison and Company, 1921). Thanks as well to Will Lucas for his essay "'Scuse Me While I Cakewalk: Carnival at the Bighouse" (http://xroads.virginia.edu/%7Eug03/lucas/cake.html).

I would like to thank my husband Paul S. Smith, who has lived with and tolerated Lacy for many years. I send thanks to the wonderful staff at Tupelo Press, especially Jim Schley for his countless hours and patience through our production, Dede Cummings and Ann Aspell for the book's design, and Nina Chanel Abney for the artwork which graces our cover and pages. I would like to send out special thanks for love, support, and guidance to Carmen Giménez Smith, Mary Gannon, Prageeta Sharma, Ronaldo Wilson, Brian Buckley, Kevin Quashie, Bhanu Kapil, Tisa Bryant, Khadija Queen, Natasha Sajé,

Douglas Kearney, Gregory Pardlo, Duriel Harris, Adrian Matejka, Ross Gay, Tyehimba Jess, Camille Dungy, A. Van Jordan, and Samiya Bashir. I extend considerable gratitude to those of my colleagues at the University of Colorado Boulder who commit to community evolution and cultural change.

OTHER BOOKS FROM TUPELO PRESS

Fasting for Ramadan: Notes from a Spiritual Practice (memoir), Kazim Ali
Fountain and Furnace (poems), Hadara Bar-Nadav
Another English: Anglophone Poems from Around the World (anthology),
    edited by Catherine Barnett and Tiphanie Yanique
Pulp Sonnets (poems, with drawings by Amin Mansouri), Tony Barnstone
gentlessness (poems), Dan Beachy-Quick
Brownwood (poems), Lawrence Bridge
The Vital System (poems), C. M. Burroughs
Everything Broken Up Dances (poems), James Byrne
One Hundred Hungers (poems), Lauren Camp
New Cathay: Contemporary Chinese Poetry (anthology), edited by Ming Di
Calazaza's Delicious Dereliction (poems), Suzanne Dracius, translated by
    Nancy Naomi Carlson
Gossip and Metaphysics: Russian Modernist Poetry and Prose (anthology),
    edited by Katie Farris, Ilya Kaminsky, and Valzhyna Mort
Entwined: Three Lyric Sequences (poems), Carol Frost
The Good Dark (poems), Annie Guthrie
Halve (poems), Kristina Jipson
Darktown Follies (poems), Amaud Jamaul Johnson
Dancing in Odessa (poems), Ilya Kaminsky
A God in the House: Poets Talk About Faith (interviews), edited by Ilya
    Kaminsky and Katherine Towler
Phyla of Joy (poems), Karen An-hwei Lee
Boat (poems), Christopher Merrill
A Camouflage of Specimens and Garments (poems), Jennifer Militello
Lucky Fish (poems), Aimee Nezhukumatathil
Weston's Unsent Letters to Modotti (poems), Chad Parmenter
Ex-Voto (poems), Adélia Prado, translated by Ellen Doré Watson
Mistaking Each Other for Ghosts (poems), Lawrence Raab
Intimate: An American Family Photo Album (hybrid memoir), Paisley Rekdal
The Book of Stones and Angels (poems), Harold Schweizer
The Well Speaks of Its Own Poison (poems), Maggie Smith
Lantern Puzzle (poems), Ye Chun

See our complete list at www.tupelopress.org